JAMES

REFORMED EXPOSITORY BIBLE STUDIES

A Companion Series to the Reformed Expository Commentaries

Series Editors

Daniel M. Doriani
Iain M. Duguid
Richard D. Phillips
Philip Graham Ryken

Daniel: Faith Enduring through Adversity
Galatians: The Gospel of Free Grace
James: Portrait of a Living Faith

JAMES

PORTRAIT OF A LIVING FAITH

A 13-LESSON STUDY

REFORMED EXPOSITORY
BIBLE STUDY

JON NIELSON

P U B L I S H I N G
P.O. BOX 817 • PHILLIPSBURG • NEW JERSEY 08865-0817

Scripture quotations in "Introducing James" and within the boxed quotations are from the HOLY BIBLE, NEW INTERNATIONAL VERSION. NIV. Copyright 1973, 1978, 1984 by International Bible Society. Used by permission of Zondervan Publishing House. All rights reserved.

Scripture quotations throughout the study or marked (ESV) are from the ESV® Bible (The Holy Bible, English Standard Version®), copyright © 2001 by Crossway, a publishing ministry of Good News Publishers. Used by permission. All rights reserved.

Italics within Scripture quotations indicate emphasis added.

All boxed quotations are taken from Daniel M. Doriani's *James* in the Reformed Expository Commentary series. Page numbers in quotations refer to that source.

ISBN: 978-1-62995-676-3 (pbk)
ISBN: 978-1-62995-677-0 (ePub)
ISBN: 978-1-62995-678-7 (Mobi)

Printed in the United States of America

CONTENTS

SERIES INTRODUCTION

Studying the Bible will change your life. This is the consistent witness of Scripture and the experience of people all over the world, in every period of church history.

King David said, "The law of the LORD is perfect, reviving the soul; the testimony of the LORD is sure, making wise the simple; the precepts of the LORD are right, rejoicing the heart; the commandment of the LORD is pure, enlightening the eyes" (Ps. 19:7–8). So anyone who wants to be wiser and happier, and who wants to feel more alive, with a clearer perception of spiritual reality, should study the Scriptures.

Whether we study the Bible alone or with other Christians, it will change us from the inside out. The Reformed Expository Bible Studies provide tools for biblical transformation. Written as a companion to the Reformed Expository Commentary, this series of short books for personal or group study is designed to help people study the Bible for themselves, understand its message, and then apply its truths to daily life.

Each Bible study is introduced by a pastor-scholar who has written a full-length expository commentary on the same book of the Bible. The individual chapters start with the summary of a Bible passage, explaining **The Big Picture** of this portion of God's Word. Then the questions in **Getting Started** introduce one or two of the passage's main themes in ways that connect to life experience. These questions may be especially helpful for group leaders in generating lively conversation.

Understanding the Bible's message starts with seeing what is actually there, which is where **Observing the Text** comes in. Then the Bible study provides a longer and more in-depth set of questions entitled **Understanding the Text**. These questions carefully guide students through the entire passage, verse by verse or section by section.

It is important not to read a Bible passage in isolation, but to see it in the wider context of Scripture. So each Bible study includes two **Bible Connections** questions that invite readers to investigate passages from other places in Scripture—passages that add important background, offer valuable contrasts or comparisons, and especially connect the main passage to the person and work of Jesus Christ.

The next section is one of the most distinctive features of the Reformed Expository Bible Studies. The authors believe that the Bible teaches important doctrines of the Christian faith, and that reading biblical literature is enhanced when we know something about its underlying theology. The questions in **Theology Connections** identify some of these doctrines by bringing the Bible passage into conversation with creeds and confessions from the Reformed tradition, as well as with learned theologians of the church.

Our aim in all of this is to help ordinary Christians apply biblical truth to daily life. **Applying the Text** uses open-ended questions to get people thinking about sins that need to be confessed, attitudes that need to change, and areas of new obedience that need to come alive by the power and influence of the Holy Spirit. Finally, each study ends with a **Prayer Prompt** that invites Bible students to respond to what they are learning with petitions for God's help and words of praise and gratitude.

You will notice boxed quotations throughout the Bible study. These quotations come from one of the volumes in the Reformed Expository Commentary. Although the Bible study can stand alone and includes everything you need for a life-changing encounter with a book of the Bible, it is also intended to serve as a companion to a full commentary on the same biblical book. Reading the full commentary is especially useful for teachers who want to help their students answer the questions in the Bible study at a deeper level, as well as for students who wish to further enrich their own biblical understanding.

The people who worked together to produce this series of Bible studies have prayed that they will engage you more intimately with Scripture, producing the kind of spiritual transformation that only the Bible can bring.

Philip Graham Ryken
Coeditor of the Reformed Expository Commentary series

INTRODUCING JAMES

James is a beloved book, since it is so practical, so full of vivid exhortations to live a godly life. In a few pages, it offers concrete counsel on an array of issues that confront Christians daily: trials, poverty, materialism, pride, favoritism, justice, planning, prayer, illness, and more.

Yet there are two sides to the book's candor and clarity. "Its call to realize professed ideals in appropriate action has spoken with prophetic urgency to generations of readers who have found James's directives difficult to perform rather than to understand."[1] The epistle of James, like the Sermon on the Mount, is sublime and penetrating—perhaps too penetrating. James stirs us to action, but as it reveals our sins, we see that we cannot do what it commands. We cannot achieve holiness or maturity by striving. Unfortunately, James declares that obedience is the hallmark of genuine faith: "Do not merely listen to the word, and so deceive yourselves. Do what it says" (1:22).

Since the author demands an obedience that we cannot render, we struggle to resolve the tension between the stringency of his demands and our failure to attain them. If this were Paul, he would turn to the work of Christ the Savior. But James never mentions the cross, the atonement, the death, or the resurrection of Jesus. He never mentions justification by faith or redemption. Indeed, the absence of these themes prompts some to wonder where redemption is found in James. James does use Jesus' name twice (James 1:1; 2:1), but in both cases there is only a passing reference to him, rather than an exposition of his person or work. Similarly, while the term *faith* appears fourteen times in James, eleven occur in 2:14–26, a discussion that stresses that faith without deeds is dead (2:17, 26). Nonetheless, James does have a gospel, and it is revealed in the broad sweep of the book.

1. Luke Timothy Johnson, *The Letter of James* (New York: Doubleday, 1995), 3.

With 59 commands in 108 verses, James presents the law of King Jesus (James 2:8). But if James merely commands, its moral clarity is a burden and its commands condemn. Yet James insists on obedience, declaring that good deeds mark true religion:

- "Religion that God our Father accepts as pure and faultless is this: to look after orphans and widows in their distress and to keep oneself from being polluted by the world" (1:27).
- "Whoever keeps the whole law but fails in one point has become accountable for all of it" (2:10, ESV).
- "Anyone, then, who knows the good he ought to do and doesn't do it, sins" (4:17).

James especially expects teachers to do what they say: "Not many of you should presume to be teachers, my brothers, because you know that we who teach will be judged more strictly" (James 3:1). This call to obey or face judgment deepens the point that no one keeps the law completely. James says we must control the tongue (1:26), yet no man can tame the tongue (3:8). He says we must avoid the pollution of the world (1:27), yet our envy and quarrels prove we are worldly (4:1–4). These paradoxes lead to the gospel. James says all are liable to judgment, but "mercy triumphs over judgment" (2:13), for "the Lord is full of compassion and mercy" (5:11). If we confess our sins, we will be healed (5:16). Further, whoever sees the sins of another and "turns a sinner from the error of his way will save him from death" (5:20).

Indeed, human inability is central to the structure of James, which hinges on three tests of true religion: "If anyone considers himself religious and yet does not keep a tight rein on his tongue, he deceives himself and his religion is worthless. Religion that God our Father accepts as pure and faultless is this: to look after orphans and widows in their distress and to keep oneself from being polluted by the world" (James 1:26–27). Notice: True religion controls the tongue, but no one can tame the tongue (3:1–12). True religion cares for the poor, but we ignore the poor or content ourselves with kind words and warm wishes (2:1–26). True religion shuns worldliness, but we all have worldly impulses (4:1–4, 13–16).

At the climax of this indictment of sin, James says that God "gives us more grace. That is why Scripture says: 'God opposes the proud but gives grace to the humble'" (James 4:6). The double mention of God's grace, just as we conclude that we fail every test of true religion, shows us the gospel of James, the message of God's grace for sinners. James's emphasis on God's word supplements this idea. The word convicts us of sin and leads to the gospel: God "chose to give us birth through the word of truth," that is, the gospel (1:18). James also says we should "humbly accept the word planted in you, which can save you" (1:21).

The **author** of James calls himself "James, a servant of God and of the Lord Jesus Christ" (James 1:1). This James is the half-brother of Jesus, the natural son of Mary and Joseph. When the author calls himself "James," without further identification, it implies that his audience already knows him so well that he can simply be "James" to them. There are three men named James in the New Testament: two apostles and the brother of Jesus. Of the apostles, the James of "Peter, James, and John" suffered martyrdom very early (Acts 12:2). At that point, James the brother of Jesus emerged in a leadership role (15:13; 21:18). (James the son of Alphaeus is unknown outside the lists of the apostles in the Gospels and Acts.)

James the brother of Jesus helped lead the Jerusalem church, making an important speech at the Council of Jerusalem. That council resolved that Gentiles, like Jews, are saved by "the grace of the Lord Jesus" (Acts 15:11). James gave the concluding speech (15:13–21).

That speech and the church's following letter (15:23–29) contain distinct language that also appears in James's epistle.[2] There is also a shared passion for the law of Moses and for peacemaking (James 2:8–11; 3:17–18; Acts 15:21, 28–29).

James had joined his brothers in mocking Jesus during his ministry. The first time John mentions Jesus's siblings, they say, "You ought to leave here and go to Judea, so that your disciples may see the miracles you do. . . . Show yourself to the world." Thus, "even his own brothers did not believe in him" (John 7:3–5). But Jesus graciously appeared to James after his resurrection (1 Cor. 15:7), and he became a pillar of the Jerusalem church.

---

2. They both include the rare use of *chairĐ* as a greeting (James 1:1; Acts 15:23), and "Listen my brothers" as an address (James 2:5; Acts 15:13). Other rare words appear in both Acts 15 and James: *episkeptesthe, epistrephein,* and *agapĐtos.*

In time, James became known as "James the Just," due to his personal righteousness and his passion to promote righteousness in others. We see the same zeal in James's epistle. He calls the law "the perfect law that gives freedom" (James 1:25) and "the royal law" (2:8). James subordinated his passion for the law to his greater passion for the gospel. James had a zeal for legal righteousness, but greater zeal for God's grace.

James's intended **audience** and the **context** of his epistle are indicated by its address to "the twelve tribes in the Dispersion" (James 1:1, ESV). The expression "the twelve tribes" traditionally signifies Israel, and "the Dispersion" refers to Jews scattered throughout the world. But James wrote especially for Jewish Christians. He was, after all, a church leader. Moreover, Paul and Peter established that the church is the true heir of God's promises to the tribes of Israel. Also, the word *dispersion* can serve as a metaphor to indicate that believers are never fully at home in this world. Peter addresses his first letter to "elect exiles of the Dispersion" (1 Peter 1:1, ESV), but it is clear that these exiles are mostly Gentiles (1:17–18; 2:11). So James envisioned a wide audience.

James assumed that his audience was familiar with life in Israel. For example, he mentions early and late rains; two rainy seasons are a distinct trait of eastern Mediterranean weather. James also refers to a synagogue (James 2:2) and assumes his audience takes pride in its monotheism (2:19). All of this implies that he is writing to people who live in the land of Israel and call Jesus "Lord" (2:1).

In short, while James surely writes for the whole church, he primarily addresses Jewish Christians. As the scribes and Pharisees demonstrate in the Gospels, there are people who know a great deal and take pride in that. But James stresses the need for knowledge that is personal and moral, not just intellectual: "You believe that God is one; you do well. Even the demons believe—and shudder!" (James 2:19, ESV). James repeatedly insists that a "faith" that has no works is useless and dead (2:17, 20, 26). So he prods theologically informed people to *live* their faith, rather than resting in doctrinal rectitude. If this summary is correct, the **purpose** of James falls into place. He both describes true faith and exposes superficial, worthless faith. Paradoxically, he says that true faith proves itself with deeds, but notes that we cannot do what we should and must therefore repent and humbly seek God's grace (4:5–10).

James mentions an array of theological themes, often briefly. His chief interest is the nature of true faith, a faith that works. He also accents God as the Lord of ethics and the Lord of our life course. These themes lead to humility, God's mercy, and the gift of rebirth. James also presents the unity of the law, creation in the image of God, and God's judgment when our brief life ends. He often reapplies teachings from the Old Testament and Jesus on such themes as trials, wisdom, wealth and poverty, speech, care for the poor, favoritism, and prayer during life's joys and sorrows.

The dominant structure of James runs from 1:26 to 4:10. There James names three tests of true religion, shows that no one can meet them, and then calls for gospel repentance. He prepares for this in 1:1–25 by showing that life constantly tests or tries everyone, whether in the form of sudden trials or ongoing challenges, such as the need to handle poverty and riches faithfully. From 4:11 to 5:20, James shows how true faith manifests itself: in humble planning, constant prayer, and care for our brothers. How blessed we students of James will be if we follow where he leads and humble ourselves before the Lord when we falter.

Daniel M. Doriani
Coeditor of the Reformed Expository Commentary series
Coeditor of the Reformed Expository Bible Study series
Author of *James* (REC)

LESSON 1

THE TRIALS OF LIFE

James 1:1–12

THE BIG PICTURE

If you have recently studied one of Paul's letters (Romans or Galatians, for example), you can be in for a bit of a jolt when you begin reading and studying the book of James. Unlike the epistles of Paul, James's entire letter mentions the name of Jesus only twice, and the substitutionary atonement is never clearly spelled out. James is chock-full of imperatives (commands). It actually reads more like a New Testament version of the Old Testament's Wisdom Literature—and in some places even like the Prophets! It's an epistle that has, at times, confounded and frustrated students and preachers who follow in the Reformed tradition, because it almost seems to ignore the central doctrines of salvation by faith alone, through grace alone. Upon careful study, though, we find that James (the half-brother of Jesus), has his theological footing carefully planted in the gospel of grace. His instructions for Jewish Christians are rooted in the hope of a God who "gives more grace" (4:6). James tells Christians to walk in step with the character of the God who, in Christ, saves sinners by his grace.

In the first twelve verses of his letter, James tackles the difficult subject of trials in the lives of Christians. He tells them to consider these trials as joy, seeing that God is at work in the midst of them to increase their godliness, maturity, and steadfastness. As believers cling to faith in God and persevere in the midst of trials, they can do so with the confidence that "the crown of life" awaits them (1:12).

Read James 1:1–12.

GETTING STARTED

1. Consider a time when you were challenged or confronted (for example, by a friend, family member, spiritual leader, or mentor) because your actions were not lining up with your words and/or beliefs. How did that person seek to convince you of your error? How did you feel when confronted? How did you respond?

2. While each of us faces different levels of trial and trouble throughout our lives, we all deal with hardship, struggles, and various forms of pain (physical, emotional, and relational). What are some of the ways in which you have sought God, in the midst of trials, over the years? What false views or perspectives on God have you had to battle as you have faced various degrees of suffering?

The Gospel of James, pg. 13
Genuine believers order their lives under the will and word of the Lord. Then, when they fail to meet the standard, they plead for grace. As James says, "Humble yourselves before the Lord, and he will lift you up" (4:10). That is the gospel of James.

OBSERVING THE TEXT

3. Begin by looking over the text carefully, observing repeated words, phrases, or ideas. As you do so, jot down your initial thoughts about the main point of these twelve verses.

4. The book of James is full of vivid imagery, metaphor, and word pictures. What vivid pictures does James use in this passage to illustrate the human subjects that he discusses? How are these images effective for us as readers?

5. Note how the passage begins and ends. What words and ideas are there in both places? How does verse 12 explain verse 2 and offer a conclusion to this section of the letter?

UNDERSTANDING THE TEXT

6. Look through James 1:1–12 and identify the main imperatives in these opening verses. What do these commands tell you about James's goal for his audience as they endure "trials of various kinds"?

7. What are the intended results of trials and testing, according to James (1:3–4)? Why does James say that his readers "know" this? Why might James not have been overly specific in his identification of these "trials," and what does this tell us about the kinds of trials he has in mind?

8. What conditions are attached to the God-intended results of trials (1:5–8)? What is necessary for us, as believers, to grow and persevere through trouble? How does James in these verses call for believers to seek wisdom, and what warnings does he offer?

The Proof of Our Faith, pg. 16

The trials of life will probe whether we live by our professed doctrines or not. James says life will try us, proving our faith authentic or inauthentic. In life's tests, abstract theology will not suffice. Genuine Christians fail some tests, of course. . . . But faithfulness during trials does prove that our faith is genuine and mature.

9. How can James 1:9–11 help us understand both poverty and wealth from a more biblical perspective? Explain James's words to both "the lowly brother" and the "rich" person. What do his commands tell us about the dangers, and the spiritual opportunities, of both situations?

10. If we understand verse 12 as the conclusion of this first section of James's letter, how does this verse confirm the main theme of these opening verses? What does this verse suggest about the reward that is ahead for believers in Christ? Who receives this reward, and what is it, exactly? How should the hope of reward motivate Christians?

BIBLE CONNECTIONS

11. The author of Hebrews, quoting from Proverbs, reminds Christians of yet another way to consider trials, pain, and trouble in this world: "My son, do not regard lightly the discipline of the Lord, nor be weary when reproved by him. For the Lord disciplines the one he loves, and chastises every son whom he receives" (Heb. 12:5b–6). How is understanding trials as potentially God's good discipline for us a helpful addition to what you have learned in James 1?

12. Proverbs 30:8–9 records a prayer for neither poverty nor riches (take a moment and read those verses now). What are the dangers and temptations that accompany material poverty? What dangers and temptations come with great wealth?

THEOLOGY CONNECTIONS

30

13. As part of the answer to the first question of the Heidelberg Catechism ("What is your only comfort in life and death?"), we find this affirmation: [Jesus] has fully paid for all my sins with his precious blood, and has set me free from the tyranny of the devil. He also watches over me in such a way that not a hair can fall from my head without the will of my Father in heaven; in fact, all things must work together for my salvation." How is this statement in agreement with the truths you've studied in James 1:1–12? How does it build upon these truths and explain more about God's care and purpose for us, even in trials?

14. Why do we face trials? Why does God allow troubles—large and small—to enter the lives of his beloved children? This passage from James that you've just studied helps to answer those difficult questions. The great Reformer, Martin Luther, wrote about one clear purpose that God has for his children in the midst of trials: In trials, God "wants to make us conformed to the image of his dear Son, Christ, so that we may become like him here in suffering and there in that life to come in

honor and glory."[1] How is this truth about God's purpose for trials an encouragement to you? What can you do to remind yourself of this in the midst of trouble or suffering?

APPLYING THE TEXT

15. James wants you to "count it all joy" when you face trials of many kinds in this life (1:2); this instruction has to do with the way you consider, think about, and understand the ordinary struggles and trials of life in a fallen world. How can you obey this command from James more joyfully and faithfully, in every season of life? What might be some practical ways in which you could grow in "counting" trials as joy, as you follow Jesus?

16. What might it look like for you to ask for "wisdom" from God in the midst of the trials of life (1:5)? Where and how might your local church fit into that process?

---

1. Martin Luther, "Sermon at Coburg on Cross and Suffering" (1530), in *Luther's Works*, vol. 51, *Sermons I*, ed. John W. Doberstein and Helmut T. Lehmann (Philadelphia: Muhlenberg Press, 1959), 206.

17. How are James's words to the poor and to the rich encouraging, challenging, or convicting to you (1:9–11)? How do these verses challenge you to embrace God's perspective on your life and your possessions?

742

PRAYER PROMPT

As you close this time of study in James 1, spend some time asking God to reshape your perspective on the ordinary trials of life, which we face in every single season. Pray that he would give you strength and humility to ask for his wisdom in the midst of trial, as your loving Father uses every trouble to build "steadfastness" in your heart and soul, for the glory of Jesus Christ.

The Life of Faith, pg. 29
The Jewish Christians who first read James needed to hear this teaching, and so do we. Many are strong in *knowledge* of the faith, but weak in the *life* of faith. James brings a corrective. The trials of life test our faith, pushing us to act, not just to think. If we withstand the tests of life, we see that our faith in Christ is genuine. Then, when God has confirmed our faith, he will grant us the crown of life eternal.

LESSON 2

BLESSED ENDURANCE

James 1:12–18

THE BIG PICTURE

James's letter began by launching into a discussion of the trials of life. These struggles can lead to faithful endurance and increasing maturity when believers turn to God and ask for wisdom (1:5). But, as we will see in James 1:12–18, struggles and trials can also be an opportunity for sinful desires to emerge—and even to sidetrack us from faithful obedience and endurance. God certainly tests his people, but he does not tempt them toward sin. Our tendency, though, can be to blame God—to accuse him of tempting us, rather than testing us—and to allow our own sinful desires to lead us away from faithful endurance in him. James's exhortation in this passage is to see the tests and trials, brought into our lives by a gracious God, as part of his good gifts to his children. He has given us life through "the word of truth" (1:18), and he will prove faithful to those who entrust themselves to him.

Read James 1:12–18.

GETTING STARTED

1. Think for a moment about friends, loved ones, or acquaintances on whom trials and struggles have had a negative spiritual effect—causing

them to question God or even turn away from him. What might James say to such people? As a result of your study of James so far, do you better understand the trials of life from a godly perspective?

2. What are some of the most difficult and/or trying experiences that you have had to endure? What did you find were some of the important keys to endurance? What were the greatest negative temptations that you faced in your quest to endure faithfully?

OBSERVING THE TEXT

3. As you most likely noticed, the verse that ended our last passage (1:12) also begins the passage for this lesson. Based on your initial reading of this passage, why might that be the case? In what ways might verse 12 serve as a hinge verse between these two sections of James's letter?

Two Ways to Take a Test, pg. 34
James knows that a test can be taken two ways. We can view it as a trial and turn to God for aid, so we persevere. Or we can read it as a tragedy, or as a senseless accident, or as a failure—on God's part—to love and protect us. Worse yet, some who meet trials blame and attack God for them, accusing him of malice. When they face tests, they do not endure, but give up.

4. Based on your first reading of this passage in James, what objections or questions does James seem to be anticipating in these verses?

5. The structure of James can be difficult to understand, but the letter does indeed have a definite shape and logical progression. Look at 1:16–18; read those three verses again. How do these verses connect to the first part of the passage (1:12–15)? What is James doing and saying in 1:16–18 in relation to what comes before?

UNDERSTANDING THE TEXT

6. What sinful and common response to trials and testing is James confronting in 1:13? How does he confront this sinful response? What does his response remind his readers about the character of God?

7. What important truths about temptation does James teach in 1:14–15? How does he explain the progression of temptation and sin? What is the final end of unrestrained sinful temptation and desire?

8. In what ways does James 1:13–16 serve as a negative counterexample to James 1:3–4 and 1:12? What sinful attitudes lead people to succumb to temptation—and ultimately death? What seem to be keys to faithful endurance in the midst of trials?

9. Why might James in 1:17 point his readers back to the goodness of God as the giver of all gifts? What spiritual gifts has the Father granted to his children? Based on what James has already explained (1:3–4, 12), how are tests and trials connected to spiritual gifts and blessings from God?

10. To what foundational truths does James call attention in 1:18? What does he mean by "the word of truth," and what word might we use interchangeably with that phrase (see Eph. 1:13 and Col. 1:5–6)?

Gifts, Not Traps, pg. 40
God is light. In him there is no darkness at all (1 John 1:5). He is the one "who does not change like shifting shadows" (James 1:17). There is no variation, no change in his goodness. Therefore, God gives good gifts, not impossible tests. We must view tests as gifts, not traps.

11. How does the word "firstfruits" in 1:18 describe the people of God? How is this verse an encouraging conclusion to this section of James's letter, following some stern warnings?

BIBLE CONNECTIONS

12. James's important distinction between testing by God and temptation by God calls our minds back to the well-known testing of Abraham in Genesis 22. Read Genesis 22:1 and then review the story of how Abraham almost sacrificed Isaac. How was this an important test of Abraham's faith? Why was it such a difficult test? How was this indeed a test of Abraham's faith, rather than God tempting him to sin?

13. In 1:18, James's chosen word for Christians (those brought forth by "the word of truth") is "firstfruits." Most likely, he has Old Testament offerings in mind here. Take a moment and read Exodus 23:19 and 34:26. What was special about the offerings of the firstfruits of God's people to him? Why should we be encouraged, as believers, that we are the "firstfruits of his creatures" in the eyes of our loving Father? How can that encourage us in the midst of trials?

THEOLOGY CONNECTIONS

14. The Westminster Confession of Faith develops more fully what James alludes to when he speaks of believers being "brought forth" by "the word of truth" (1:18). In chapter 10 ("Of Effectual Calling"), we find that God graciously chooses "effectually to call, by his Word and Spirit, out of that state of sin and death, in which they are by nature, to grace and salvation, by Jesus Christ; enlightening their minds spiritually and savingly to understand the things of God" (10.1). How is this a helpful explanation of our salvation? In what way does this phrase further point to God as the great gift-giver?

15. William Tyndale, an early Reformer who was ultimately martyred, once penned these words: "The Spirit and his fruits wherewith the heart is purified, as faith, hope, love, patience, longsuffering and obedience, could never be seen without outward experience. For if you were not brought sometime into cumbrance, when God only could deliver you, you would never see your faith" ("The Obedience of a Christian Man," 1528). How do his words further explain tests and trials as part of God's good gifts to his children?

APPLYING THE TEXT

16. In the passage you've studied in this lesson, James has reminded us of a key distinction: God may *test* his people, but he will not *tempt* them

to sin. Why is this such a key distinction to remember? How is this helpful to you personally? How does this help you to grow in your understanding of God's fatherly love for you?

17. Based on James's strong warnings in this passage (especially in 1:13–16), how can you guard and watch your heart in the midst of trials? What sinful tendencies must you avoid, and how can you be on your guard against them?

18. Why is it so important for us as believers to remember that our God is the ultimate giver of all good gifts? How can reminders of his character—his grace, mercy, and generosity—strengthen us in the midst of trial?

God's Gift, pg. 41

This is the kindness and excellence of God. As the gospel wins the hearts of sinners, they freely choose the new life that he already willed for them. Because our life rests on God's unchanging goodness, not our own changeable choices, it is secure. That is God's gift; it proves his good intent in our trials.

PRAYER PROMPT

As you close your study of James 1:12–18, spend some time in prayer to the Giver of all good gifts. Thank him for giving you spiritual birth through his "word of truth." Praise him for graciously loving you as a "firstfruit" among all his creatures. Ask him for strength to see your trials as tests—and even "gifts"—from a God who loves you and will give you grace to endure faithfully.

LESSON 3

HEARING TO OBEY

James 1:19–25

THE BIG PICTURE

James has been calling his readers toward joyful, Word-grounded endurance in the midst of the trials and troubles of life. Now his exhortation will continue on the theme of the Word of God—specifically, the right response to hearing it. How can a Christian know that he or she is hearing God's Word rightly? How can followers of Christ be sure that the Word of God is truly "implanted" deeply and savingly in their souls (1:21)? James's answer is simple: we can look for evidence of actively obeying the Word. A putting off of sin and a yearning for the Word will result in a rejection of sinful anger and speech (1:19–21). Those with genuine belief in God as revealed in the Word will not just listen to it, but reorder their lives around it and seek to obey it actively (1:22). True believers will allow the Word to expose—and change—sinful tendencies in their hearts and lives (much like a powerful mirror), as they know more and more the blessings that come with true hearing and obedience (1:23–25).

Read James 1:19–25.

GETTING STARTED

1. Have you ever heard someone, but not really *listened* to them? Perhaps you can think of a time when you heard words that your parent, coach,

teacher, spouse, or friend spoke to you—but you didn't intentionally act on what they said to you. Why would that be frustrating for the one speaking the words, making the request, or giving the advice?

2. One metaphor for the Word of God in this passage is "a mirror" (1:23). What are the benefits of a mirror? Why do people use them? What unfortunate realities can mirrors sometimes expose?

OBSERVING THE TEXT

3. Look through the passage, particularly noting the contrasts that James identifies in these verses. What different kinds of people, approaches to the Word, and attitudes about life does he contrast?

Questions for the Soul, pg. 55

James questions his readers: Has the word been implanted in you? Has it saved your soul? Do you persevere with the word and with the Lord who spoke it? He also commands: If the word is implanted in you, let it show.

4. As we mentioned above, James speaks of the Word of God in this passage being like "a mirror." Why is that a helpful metaphor? What does he imply about the Word of God (and about ourselves) by using a mirror as a metaphor?

5. Based on your initial reading of the passage, what are some of the issues that you think James may be confronting in the lives—and perhaps the church—of his audience? Why do you think this?

UNDERSTANDING THE TEXT

6. In James 1:19–20, what important truths are being taught about human anger, as well as angry speech? In what practical ways can this teaching be helpful to everyone? How is it particularly important for the follower of Jesus?

7. In James 1:21, the command to "put away" sin precedes the command to "receive" the word. Why might the order of those commands be surprising to us? Does the order seem to be reversed? What is the best explanation for this?

8. What does James mean that the implanted word is "able to save your souls" (1:21)? What does this mean theologically? How should this reality shape our approach to ministry and life in the church, and affect our relationships?

9. Why does James speak of deception in 1:22? In what ways is self-deception present and active in a Christian faith that does not involve active obedience?

The Work of the Implanted Word, pg. 48

We notice that James, unlike Paul, does not tell believers to put off sins and to put on certain virtues. He says "receive the implanted word," not "work at removing sin." This is how transformation occurs: The implanted word takes root deep within us and transforms us. It brings conviction of sin and assurance of mercy. It instills faith and creates new life, so that good fruit inevitably follows.

10. What do we learn about the Word of God through James's extended metaphor in 1:23–24? What do we learn about our own sinful tendencies and temptations with regard to God's Word? In what ways might Scripture illuminate certain aspects of our lives and hearts that we may want to forget?

11. How does verse 25 offer a conclusion to this section of James's letter? What themes are repeated? Why might the idea of blessing have been introduced in this verse, and why is that significant?

BIBLE CONNECTIONS

12. While many throughout history have sought to pit James against Paul, there would certainly be no disagreement from Paul about James's strong assertions in the passage we have been studying. Romans 2:13 declares: "For it is not the hearers of the law who are righteous before God, but the doers of the law who will be justified." Whom might Paul have in mind as he writes those words, given his context and the context of the epistle to the Romans?

13. Read Psalm 1:1–2. How is the blessing of Psalm 1 echoed by the blessing promised in James 1:25? What similar approaches and attitude toward God's Word emerge from Psalm 1 and James 1?

THEOLOGY CONNECTIONS

14. John Knox, sometimes referred to as "the Father of Scottish Presbyterianism," once said: "Study to practice in life that which the Lord commands, and then be you assured that you shall never hear nor read the same without fruit" ("A Most Wholesome Counsel," 1556). How does Knox's exhortation relate to what you have studied in James 1? What does this approach to Scripture imply about the right study of God's Word and its application in daily life?

15. Speaking of the role of good works and obedience in the Christian life, the Westminster Confession of Faith states: "These good works, done in obedience to God's commandments, are the fruits and evidences of a true and lively faith: and by them believers manifest their thankfulness, strengthen their assurance, edify their brethren, adorn the profession of the gospel, stop the mouths of the adversaries, and glorify God, whose workmanship they are, created in Christ Jesus thereunto, that, having their fruit unto holiness, they may have the end, eternal life" (16.2). In

what ways is the WCF agreeing with James's call to active obedience to the Word of God, rather than just an unmoved "hearing" of the Word?

APPLYING THE TEXT

16. Consider your own faith journey and/or conversion story. In what way did your desire to put away certain aspects of your life perhaps precede your actual faith in the gospel and God's Word? How might you apply this to your approach to sharing the good news of the gospel with your family and friends?

17. Describe some ways in which the Bible has acted like a mirror for your soul by revealing sinful thoughts, tendencies, words, or actions. How can you actively allow God's Word to continue doing that in your life? What attitude do you need to adopt as you read the Bible or sit under biblical teaching?

A Mirror for the Soul, pg. 53

As a mirror shows physical flaws, so the word is a mirror for the soul. It shows moral and spiritual flaws so that we can remedy them. But to profit from Scripture as a mirror, we must remember what we see and act accordingly.

18. How can you tell if you are *hearing* parts of God's Word without actively *obeying* them? In what ways might the local church and Christian community help you with this kind of discernment?

PRAYER PROMPT

As you end your time of studying this passage, prayerfully allow this portion of God's Word to act as a mirror for your heart and soul. Ask God to expose areas of sin and selfishness that need to change. Pray that he would help you to stare intently at his Word—with a willingness to repent and actively grow in obedience and the blessing of holiness. Consider inviting others to study God's Word with you and pray in similar ways.

LESSON 4

THE TESTS OF TRUE RELIGION

James 1:26–2:7

THE BIG PICTURE

The word *religion* is often used with a negative connotation in our culture today. Even among committed Christians, there has been a recent move toward contrasting "religion" with the true gospel, which involves a *relationship* with Jesus, rather than a set of religious rituals or rules. For James, though, *religion* is not a dirty word; in fact, true religion, when rightly lived out, is a beautiful picture of the character of God. In the passage you will study today, James begins by laying out some foundational tests of true religion, which have to do with our speech, our interaction with those who are vulnerable and needy, and our moral and mental purity in our sinful world. James then goes on to describe another sign of true Christian religion: a lack of favoritism or partiality on the basis of wealth or appearance. Such favoritism would be, according to James, starkly in contrast with the heart of a God who has chosen "those who are poor in the world to be rich in faith and heirs of the kingdom" (2:5). Especially in the context of the church, there must be no partiality; true Christian religion precludes any such favoritism.

Read James 1:26–2:7.

GETTING STARTED

1. Consider a time when you were *tested*, in some formal way, in order to see if you were ready or fit for a position or responsibility. What was the test trying to determine? Why did the administrators of the test consider it to be important? How did the test connect with the position or responsibility you desired?

2. In what ways you have observed wealthy people getting special treatment, gaining access to unique privileges, or receiving extra honor or respect from others? How have you seen this reality played out in the context of the Christian community, Christian organizations, or the local church? Why is this so dangerous?

The Proof of Our Religion, pg. 58

To this day, religious people may profess orthodox doctrines and faithfully attend their churches. But the proof of their religion lies in behavior, James says. He unfolds the meaning of these marks of true religion—controlling the tongue, caring for the needy, and shunning the world's pollution—throughout chapters 2–4.

OBSERVING THE TEXT

3. As this passage opens, notice the first indication of true religion that James mentions. Why might James start with talking about the tongue? If you've read the book of James in its entirety, can you point to places where he talks about the tongue later in the letter?

4. Upon your first reading of this text, how would you characterize James's tone as he writes these verses? How would you imagine him speaking these words to his readers?

5. What is convicting and confrontational in this passage? Which rebukes and exhortations are most humbling to you personally as you first read it through? Why is this?

UNDERSTANDING THE TEXT

6. According to James's words in 1:26–27, there are at least three tests of true religion (one negative and two positive). What are they? Which is

the negative test, and which two are the positive tests? Are you surprised by any of these tests that James chooses to identify here? If so, why?

7. Why might James count care for widows and orphans as a key test of true religion? In what ways would those who fit that description have been particularly vulnerable—especially in James's historical context?

8. In your own words, what does James mean by his call to remain "unstained from the world"? From what you know of other parts of Scripture, what do biblical writers mean by "the world"? If James is not teaching an extreme separationist view, what exactly is he teaching?

The Sin of Favoritism, pg. 63

Favoritism is utterly worldly. It continues the world's inclination to prefer the rich over the poor. Favoritism rejects God's decision to grant equal honor to the poor and the rich. Favoritism forgets God's will and seeks the favor of the rich by giving them special attention.

9. Why might showing favoritism, or "partiality," in the context of the local church be a strongly negative indication of one's true faith in God (2:1)? How does favoritism, especially on the basis of wealth or influence, do damage to the message of the gospel of Jesus Christ? What false values and patterns of thinking would such partiality reveal in the hearts and minds of those in the church who practice it?

10. How is James's illustration of a rich man and a poor man wearing very different clothing (2:2–4) particularly effective in making his point? Why is this story so powerful?

11. How does James, in 2:5, explain why favoritism on the basis of wealth and appearance violates the heart of true religion? What does he remind his audience about God and about God's way of working his salvation in the world? What does he remind them about the ways that the rich and powerful in our world often act?

BIBLE CONNECTIONS

12. James's teaching about the importance (and danger) of the ton;
    just one way that his epistle connects well with the Wisdom Liter
    of the Old Testament. Take a moment and read Proverbs 10:19
    one example of the teaching in Proverbs concerning restraining
    tongue). How is the wisdom of Proverbs 10:19 reflected in the op
    verses of the passage in James that you have studied today?

13. Many scholars have pointed to echoes of the teachings of Jesus in
    book of James. Read Matthew 5:3, which includes Jesus' teaching;
    "the poor in spirit." How are Jesus' declarations echoed in what Ja
    says about the poor in James 2:5? In what ways might James's teach
    be based on other aspects of Jesus' Sermon on the Mount?

THEOLOGY CONNECTIONS

14. Jonathan Edwards, the early American pastor, writer, and theologi;
    famously made a long list of resolutions. One of those resolutions rea(
    "Resolved, never to say anything at all against anybody, but when it
    perfectly agreeable to the highest degree of Christian honor, and
    love to mankind, agreeable to the lowest humility, and sense of my ov
    faults and failings, and agreeable to the golden rule; often, when I ha
    said anything against anyone, to bring it to, and try it strictly by tl

test of this Resolution" (Resolution 31, 1772). How is this resolution a faithful and legitimate application of James 1:26?

15. In systematic theology, the phrase *total depravity* is often used to describe the absolute fallenness of every human being, as well as the complete inability of anyone in his or her sinful state to please or choose God apart from the work of the Holy Spirit. How does the doctrine of total depravity connect with a call to avoid favoritism? How can favoritism toward some types of people functionally deny this doctrine?

APPLYING THE TEXT

16. As you consider the tests of true religion laid out in James 1:26–27, how do you measure up? What is your honest assessment of your use of your tongue? Are there ways in which you are seeking to care for those around you who are particularly vulnerable? How do you seek to live in the world and yet be "unstained" by it? What goals might you set for yourself in these key areas of testing?

17. How have you been guilty of showing partiality or favoritism on the basis of wealth, popularity, power, or influence? When you observe sinful favoritism in the Christian community, how might you begin to confront it?

18. In what ways does God's heart for the poor need to better shape your approach to those in your church community? What might that look like in practical terms?

PRAYER PROMPT

This is a passage—like many in James's letter—that can fill even the most committed Christians with self-doubt, strong conviction, and a deep sense of failure. None of us completely and perfectly passes all of James's tests for true religion! As you pray to close this time of study, ask God to help you—by the power of the Holy Spirit—to grow and mature in all of the areas that James identifies in this passage. Also, praise God for providing his Son to cover your sins, pass the test in your place, and save you forever.

The One Who Passed Our Tests, pg. 67
Because we sin daily, we need to repent again, ask for grace again, and rest in the gospel again. We will never pass all the tests. Thank God, Jesus has passed them for us and made us members of his family. In the gospel, he has cared for us in our poverty and distress.

LESSON 5

ALL OR NOTHING

James 2:8–13

THE BIG PICTURE

As you saw in the last chapter, there are some sure tests that we can use on ourselves in order to see if we really are living out "true religion" as we follow the Lord Jesus Christ. While our ultimate hope is not in our own perfection, but that of Christ's in our place, we nevertheless are called to grow in the areas that James identifies—the use of our tongues, our care for the poor and vulnerable, our purity in the midst of a crooked world, and our God-centered rejection of all forms of favoritism. Now, in James 2:8–13, James continues to lay out a picture of full devotion to God and obedience to his Word. The true follower of Jesus is committed to the love of neighbor completely, as well as the avoidance of murder (and hatred) and adultery (and lust). There are no insignificant or trivial aspects of God's commands; our calling as Christians is to speak and act as those with total devotion to the Word of God in every way. Even as we put our hope in the mercy of a gracious God, we are called to strive vigorously after total, complete, and wholehearted obedience to that merciful God. He saves us, and he demands *all* of us!

Read James 2:8–13.

GETTING STARTED

1. What are some examples of situations, results, or commitments in life that you would consider to be "all or nothing" (that is, with no potential for merely *partial* success or failure)?

2. In what ways do you normally think about the idea of "all or nothing" applying to your spiritual life or your walk with God? How do you often *not* include an "all or nothing" idea in your thinking about your Christian life?

OBSERVING THE TEXT

3. How would you describe James's tone in these verses? Do you detect hints of irony—or tongue-in-cheek ways of speaking—at any points in this passage (for example, in 2:8)? If so, where—and what might James be trying to accomplish?

All or Nothing Obedience, pg. 69

"All or nothing" seems like the wrong category [for obedience]. After all, we are tempted daily and sometimes succumb, so we would say we try to obey God, but find only partial success. . . . Yet James 2 says there is a sense in which obedience is all or nothing.

4. How many references to the Old Testament law—both specifically and generally—does James make in these six verses? Why is that significant?

5. As you first read through this passage, how did you see verse 13 connecting with the previous verses? How does this idea of mercy and judgment flow out of what James has been saying? In what ways does this verse make sense as a concluding thought to this section of the letter?

UNDERSTANDING THE TEXT

6. How do verses 8–9 continue James's teaching on favoritism and partiality—and the dangers of both? What do these verses add to the discussion, and how does James ground his teaching in the law of God?

7. Read James 2:10 again, slowly, and consider this massive statement from James. Why is this verse surprising and unexpected? In what ways is this statement contrary to what most people think, concerning religious devotion, in your culture today? What does this verse teach us about the character of God?

8. How does 2:11 further explain and demonstrate the point that James is making in 2:10? What potential danger is he exposing in a potential attitude and approach to the law of God?

9. In what ways might 2:10–11 drive us to our knees and confront us with our desperate need for Jesus? How are these verses deeply humbling and convicting? In what ways is the gospel of Jesus Christ the refreshing hope for those convicted by these verses?

10. What does James assert about "judgment" in 2:12? On what basis will we all be judged, according to James, and why is this important? Why must every Christian understand this truth?

Obeying God Himself, pg. 74

If we pick and choose among the commands, we never really obey *God himself*. If we follow only the laws we like, if we obey laws that we find agreeable, we make ourselves the final arbiter of truth. . . . In this way, obedience is all or nothing. We submit to God totally or not at all.

11. While James speaks frankly about judgment, he does not speak of judgment unaccompanied by mercy. What is encouraging about his mention of "mercy" in 2:13? What does he say about the "mercy" of God? Why is this a deeply encouraging conclusion to this passage, and how does it relate to the work of Jesus Christ?

BIBLE CONNECTIONS

12. Perhaps the most surprising aspect of Jesus' teaching in the Sermon on the Mount (especially to his original Jewish listeners) was his elevated call to obedience, righteousness, and even perfection—with regard to God's law. Read Matthew 5:21–26, for example, and note how Jesus takes the prohibition against murder to a much deeper, more internal place. How do James's words in 2:10–11 echo the teaching of Jesus in Matthew 5? What connections do you observe between the two passages?

13. The ominous reality of God's judgment on the guilty, which hangs over James 2:10–12, can fill us with great fear. Yet according to Psalm 130:4, it is also God's "forgiveness" that is meant to fill us with fear. Why should the prospect of God's *mercy*, as well as his *judgment*, cause us to fear and worship him with reverence, joy, and submission?

THEOLOGY CONNECTIONS

14. In the Westminster Confession of Faith, all men and women are called to repent, mindful of this fact: "As there is no sin so small, but it deserves damnation; so there is no sin so great, that it can bring damnation upon those who truly repent" (15.4). How does this affirmation summarize well James's teachings about the importance of obedience to the whole law of God, but also about the triumph of God's mercy?

15. Augustine of Hippo once asserted, "If you believe what you like in the gospels, and reject what you don't like, it is not the gospel you believe, but yourself." Based on what you have studied in James 2:8–13, why do you think James would have enthusiastically agreed with this comment?

APPLYING THE TEXT

16. As you carefully consider your own spiritual life, in what areas might you detect an attitude of partial obedience or a tendency to pick and choose which commands of God you will obey? How can you confront this dangerous tendency? In what ways might you be alerted to a lack of complete submission to God?

17. When we are confronted with our sin and failure, we can be tempted to try to solve our problems in ways other than by genuine repentance and trust in the mercy of God. What are your sinful tendencies when you are confronted with your sin and failure in obedience? Do you resort to simply trying harder? Do you give in to shame and despair? Do you tend to deny your sin?

18. In what practical ways might you contribute to a church community that is serious about total obedience to God, while also resting deeply in the mercy of God—in Christ—for salvation?

God's Great Grace, pg. 78

If we reject a command because it is unpalatable, we have rejected the Lord who gave that law. . . . Still, God's grace is greater than our sin. The gospel goes to *sinners*, to the unworthy, to the poor in spirit. The Lord is pleased when we obey, yet for all who repent and believe, he loves and forgives even when we fail him.

PRAYER PROMPT

It is impossible for anyone who is earnestly and humbly studying James
2:8–13 to avoid falling under the conviction of sin, failure, and judgment.
No one keeps the law of God perfectly. Thankfully, James points his readers
to the mercy of God, which triumphs over judgment. As you close your
study of this passage with prayer, confess sin honestly and openly to God.
Ask him for strength to resist picking and choosing what you will obey in
his Word; beg him to give you an undivided heart to obey him. Finally,
thank him for the mercy of Jesus Christ, who perfectly kept the law of God
and died in the place of lawbreakers.

LESSON 6

FAITH THAT WORKS

James 2:14–19

THE BIG PICTURE

James has already spent quite a bit of time developing an important, convicting, assertion: true religion demonstrates itself in obedience and good works. Faith—real faith—will make a difference in the way we speak, the way we listen to God's Word, the way we endure trials, and the way we reject favoritism and partiality. Now, though, James becomes even more provocative, as he takes on a kind of "faith" that cannot truly save. This non-saving faith, according to James, is composed of mental assent to the truths about God found in his Word, but has absolutely no impact on the lives and works of those who hold it. This kind of faith, in fact, is "dead" (2:17). In support of his provocative claim, James offers two examples of ineffective (and thus "dead") faith in the passage you will study today. The first example shows empty words that are offered to a person in need, rather than generous actions; the second offers a picture of the kind of non-saving faith that even Satan's demons possess! Clearly, *saving* faith, according to James, will bear fruit in good works—love for God and neighbor.

Read James 2:14–19.

GETTING STARTED

1. Without mentioning names, can you describe your interactions and/or experiences with people who seemed to hold to an orthodox view of God, sin, and salvation—but who did not live out Christian faith or morality? How did they justify their behavior? What seemed to be missing in their hearts and minds?

2. What definitions of *faith* have you heard that seem deficient? Explain some examples that you've heard of "easy believism"—the teaching that you just need to "believe" in Jesus and you will go to heaven. Why must our definitions of *faith* and *belief* involve, at least at some level, a reference to obedience and transformed lives?

The Faith That Does Not Save, pg. 81

James begins the process with a question: "What good is it . . . my brothers, if someone says he has faith but does not have works? Can that faith save him?" . . . [This] is a contemporary question. When James faces it, he answered directly. There is a "faith" that does not save. It is the faith that adheres to orthodox theology but has no actions.

OBSERVING THE TEXT

3. As you look carefully at this text, note James's use of questions. How many questions does he ask his readers in these verses? What kinds of questions does he ask? Why is this method of teaching effective, particularly in this passage?

4. How are James's examples of the poorly clothed brother or sister and of the demons effective in making his point?

5. What is initially surprising, or even shocking, in this passage? Why might James's way of wording certain phrases concern many Christians who hold to salvation by "faith alone"?

UNDERSTANDING THE TEXT

6. In 2:14, James points to the insufficiency *for salvation* of a certain kind of faith, when he asks, "Can that faith save him?" Is James questioning the doctrine of salvation by faith? Why or why not? If not, what is he affirming quite strongly in this verse?

7. What comments does James's imaginary character make to the brother or sister who is lacking food and clothing (2:15–16)? What attitude seems to lurk behind these comments? What does this person "who says he has faith" fail to do?

8. What point is James making in 2:17 about "faith by itself"? Does such faith actually exist? Describe in your own words what such a kind of "faith" might look like in today's context.

9. What motivation seems to be behind the objection that James anticipates in 2:18? In what way does this objection seek to make a separation that James immediately rejects as invalid?

Useless Faith, pg. 85

A faith that ostensibly unites a believer to the family of God, but does nothing that actually benefits his fellow believers, is useless and dead (2:17). Those who have such faith fail the second test of true religion. They have no true love of God.

10. How would you characterize the belief of the demons in God, which James mentions in 2:19? In what sense do they "believe" in God? What do they lack, as part of this belief?

11. What in this passage seems objectionable—or dangerous—to you? Why do you think that is the case? What reactions does James intend to draw out from his audience?

BIBLE CONNECTIONS

12. As we have already seen in the book of James, the words of Jesus often seem to be echoed. Read Matthew 25:31–46. How does Jesus' convicting teaching in this passage seem to shape James's teaching in James 2:15–16?

13. Many have contrasted James's epistle with the writings of the apostle Paul on justification by faith alone. In Romans 3:28, for example, Paul asserts very clearly that we are "justified by faith apart from works of the law." What does Paul mean by "apart from"? What is Paul teaching,

exactly, and how does it agree with what James is teaching in our passage (see the beginning of Romans 6, for example)?

THEOLOGY CONNECTIONS

14. While James does not use the word *grace* in this passage, his teaching relates closely to orthodox rejections of "cheap grace." Dietrich Bonhoeffer, the twentieth-century German theologian, once wrote: "Cheap grace is the preaching of forgiveness without requiring repentance, baptism without church discipline, Communion without confession, absolution without personal confession. Cheap grace is grace without discipleship, grace without the cross, grace without Jesus Christ, living and incarnate" (*The Cost of Discipleship*, 1937). How might you use James 2:14–19 to confront those who embrace "cheap grace"—the acceptance of forgiveness from God without any commitment to discipleship and obedience?

15. Martin Luther, who famously struggled with the book of James, nevertheless stated: "Faith alone makes someone just and fulfills the law. . . . Faith is that which brings the Holy Spirit through the merits of Christ" (introduction to *Romans*, 1522). In what ways does the doctrine of the indwelling Holy Spirit in believers support James's teaching in 2:14–19? How is a consideration of the Holy Spirit helpful in this discussion?

APPLYING THE TEXT

16. James 2:15–16 describes a scene in which a person of "faith" fails to extend practical help to someone in need, even as the refusal is cloaked in religious and spiritual language. How have you seen religious language used to justify sin or a failure to do good? Have you ever done this? If so, how?

17. In what ways might you be able to tell whether or not you are merely giving mental assent to Christian truths or actually living a life of costly discipleship, obedience, and good works? Can you point to any evidence in your life of saving and changing faith?

18. How can some church contexts contribute to the formation of dead faith, which involves orthodox views and unchanged lives? In what ways might local churches seek to address this problem and avoid this danger?

The Good News, pg. 88
James's critique of false faith feels like bad news. But . . . there is good news too. Real faith does express itself in acts of love. It does care for the needy. Christians do not simply grit their teeth and resolve to keep more laws. New behavior flows from a new heart.

PRAYER PROMPT

As you complete your time of study in this convicting and provocative passage from James, it will be good to search your own heart and soul for evidence of faith that is living and active. James means to frighten and shake up complacent people of faith—some of whom may be in danger of possessing merely orthodox assertions, rather than active Christian obedience. Pray that God would make your living faith more and more evident in your obedience, your generosity, your holiness, and your love for brothers and sisters in Christ. Ask him to transform you more and more into the likeness of Jesus as you look to him in true faith.

LESSON 7

JUSTIFIED BY A
FAITH THAT WORKS

James 2:20–26

THE BIG PICTURE

In the verses leading up to the ones you will study today, James provocatively identifies a kind of "faith" that is actually not a saving faith. This "no good" faith consists of merely mental assent and orthodox assertions, without any actions or obedience; it's the kind of "faith" that even the demons hold! Now, in 2:20–26, James continues his argument—citing two more examples for his point. First, James puts forward Abraham, who was "justified" through the obedient work of offering his son Isaac up to God as a sacrifice. Second, James reminds his audience of Rahab, who was "justified by works" in the way she feared God and helped the Hebrew spies in Jericho. For both Abraham and Rahab, James's point is that any "faith" they claimed to possess would not have been true faith if it had not produced real works of obedience. It is this kind of active, obedient, living faith that justifies—not an inactive faith of mere assent to claims of truth about God.

Read James 2:20–26.

GETTING STARTED

1. Give some examples in everyday life where merely *affirming* something with words bears no weight unless that affirmation is *acted* upon. In what ways do our actions give more weight to our affirmations—and even prove the affirmations to be true?

2. What are some of the ways in which you have heard people describe their hope that God will accept them because of what they have done? Has someone ever told you that they would go to heaven because they are a good person? How did they articulate this hope, based on their life and beliefs?

OBSERVING THE TEXT

3. Upon your initial reading of this passage, what is most striking to you? What are the surprises in the text?

True Religion Works, pg. 91

Remember that James is on a quest for true religion, not the religion that simply says, "God is one" (2:19) and affirms the elements of the orthodox theology. True religion *works*. It hears and obeys.

4. How would you describe James's tone as the passage begins (note 2:20)? Why would you describe it that way? Why might James have been writing these words with such force and conviction? What problems in the church was he perhaps confronting?

5. As you surely noticed, James uses the phrase "justified by works" several times in this passage. What is your immediate reaction to that phrase? Why do most evangelical Christians avoid using that phrase?

UNDERSTANDING THE TEXT

6. Why does James describe faith apart from works as "useless" (2:20)? To *whom* is it useless (see 2:21–23)? What is this teaching us about true faith and about God?

7. James 2:22 says that Abraham's "faith was completed by his works." What is James teaching about Abraham's obedience? In what way would

his faith *not* have been completed, had he not obeyed God's command regarding Isaac?

8. How do verses 23–24 conclude James's lesson from the life of Abraham? How might you use verses 21–24 to critique a definition of *faith* that does not include actions, obedience, or a life of service to God?

9. Using James 2:20–24, how would you explain the connection between Abraham's faith in God and his obedience to God? To use a different word, how did Abraham's works *vindicate* him as someone who had truly put his faith in God?

10. Abraham's obedient works were directed toward God, as vindication of his true faith. But toward whom were Rahab's good works directed (2:25–26)? What important truths can we learn from this?

11. How was Rahab's help of the Hebrew spies inextricably linked to her genuine faith in God? If she had not helped them, what would that have

said about her faith? Would Rahab's faith in God have been evident, or even genuine, apart from her actions?

BIBLE CONNECTIONS

12. Genesis 15:6 (which describes Abraham's belief in God, and God's counting him as righteous) is quoted many times in the New Testament as evidence for salvation coming through faith alone. How does Genesis 15:6 relate to Genesis 22 (Abraham's obedient, near sacrifice of Isaac)? How do Abraham's obedient actions prove and justify the real faith that he had placed in God so many years earlier?

13. Many Christians point to Ephesians 2:1–10 as a beautiful summary of the gospel work of God in the lives of sinners—sinners who are "dead" in their sins, apart from Christ, and unable to choose God on their own. Read Ephesians 2:10, though, again. What does Paul include here as part of God's purpose in our salvation by grace? How does this connect to James's teaching in the passage you've been studying?

The Vitality of Faith, pg. 93

James is aware that Genesis 15 teaches justification by faith; he cites the passage in James 2:23. Even if James wrote his epistle before Paul wrote Galatians and Romans (as many scholars believe), he knows that Paul taught justification by faith. He knows Abraham looked at the stars, believed, and thus was justified before God. But James also knows that Abraham's faith demonstrated its vitality by its works.

THEOLOGY CONNECTIONS

14. For Augustine of Hippo, a "faith" with no accompanying obedience would not only be dead, but also a sign that the Spirit-given enjoyment of God had not gripped one's heart and transformed one's affections. "How sweet all at once it was for me to be rid of those fruitless joys which I had once feared to lose," he wrote. "You drove them from me and took their place" (*Confessions*, 9.1). Given this understanding of what happens when a person is saved, why would the idea of faith apart from works be all the more illogical?

15. The Heidelberg Catechism says that a believer in Jesus is "duty-bound to use his gifts readily and cheerfully for the benefit and well-being of the other members" (Q&A 55). How did Rahab live out this duty of a true believer? What is challenging about this call for us as Christians today?

APPLYING THE TEXT

16. Most likely, you have received solid teaching about eternal salvation from God coming through faith alone—apart from your own good works. How, though, have you seen tendencies in your own life and

heart to abuse this reality and minimize the importance of good works and obedience?

17. What effect ought James's teaching in this passage to have on your motivation with regard to good works and obedience to God? If good works are not to be done in order to earn you saving favor with God (which comes only through the work of Christ), why should you seek to obey God?

18. As we saw in James 2:20–26, genuine faith is pleasing to God (Abraham). But genuine faith is also helpful to God's people (Rahab). How might you better evaluate your service, generosity, and humility toward others, in order to test the genuineness of your faith?

The Believer Adds Nothing, pg. 95
When we say a believer is justified by faith alone, we mean that the believer adds nothing—no works—*in order to earn* or gain God's favor. Good works *are* necessary—not a condition prior to salvation but a consequence following salvation.

PRAYER PROMPT

James 2:20–26 has called us to consider the integral and inescapable connection between faith in God and lives of good works and service to both God and others. Any faith that is not vindicated through obedience is not just deficient, but "dead" (2:26)! Today, as you close your time of study in God's Word, ask him to convict you of ways that you tend toward faith apart from works. Ask him to graciously allow your faith in Jesus to be vindicated—more and more—in humble obedience to his Word and joyful service to those around you.

LESSON 8

WHO CAN TAME THE TONGUE?

James 3:1–12

THE BIG PICTURE

James has mentioned before—briefly—the importance of control of one's tongue. In 1:26, he declared that the one who practices true religion must "bridle his tongue." Now, though, James lays out extensive teachings and warnings about the dangerous, fiery weapon that we all can wield: our words. Using vivid pictures and illustrations from nature and the technology of his day, James explains the stunning power and explosive influence of the tongue—both of which are disproportionate to its size in comparison with the body. The tongue is so powerful that James will even suggest that if someone were to completely tame his or her words and speech, that person would be perfect (3:2)! The reason for this is that the tongue reflects the inner workings of the heart; human words are an overflow of the deepest realities of the soul. This is why, according to James, those who practice true religion must seek to guard their hearts—and also their tongues, which reflect their hearts. Far too often, even for "religious" people, speech can be full of praises to God in one moment and filled with cursing others in the next (3:10).

Read James 3:1–12.

GETTING STARTED

1. Think of some examples from your life when words did serious damage, even if the person who spoke them did not mean serious harm. How have you seen people's tongues do incredible damage to relationships, communities, or organizations?

2. In what ways does someone's speech—the specific words they choose, their way of speaking, or even their tone—reveal so much about their character? What judgments do you make about people because of the way they talk?

The Tongue's Influence, pg. 108

The tongue is most influential. As a bit directs a horse and a rudder directs a ship, so the tongue directs human life. What we *do* follows what we *say*. Both our internal speech (our thoughts) and our spoken words direct our actions.

OBSERVING THE TEXT

3. As we have seen, James is a master of metaphor and word pictures. How is this true in James 3:1–12? What specific pictures does James use to show what the power and danger of the tongue can be like?

4. Why are the particular images and illustrations that James uses so powerful? How do they support his teachings and warnings?

5. In what ways is the reader warned by James in this passage? How do these warnings connect to what James has already said about the relationship between faith and works?

UNDERSTANDING THE TEXT

6. James begins this passage, in 3:1–2, by issuing a warning to those who teach, before discussing the dangers of the tongue for the remaining ten

verses. What is the connection between the "teacher" and the "tongue"? Explain the logical progression that causes James to move from 3:1–2 to 3:3–12.

7. Given the three specific pictures that James uses to describe the tongue in 3:3–5, what truths are we supposed to grasp about the tongue? Explain the unique contribution that each comparison offers to our understanding of the danger and power of our words.

8. James 3:6 is packed with particularly insightful teaching about the tongue. What does this verse remind us about the tongue's role in evil? What do we learn about the tongue's influence? In what sense can the tongue be linked with "hell" itself?

Watching Our Words, pg. 113
Notice that James chides our inconsistency, even though he knows no one can consistently control the tongue. He rebukes us because the duty of watching our words remains. Since a small statement can cause great harm, we must guard our speech. We must strive to bless God and mankind with our tongues.

9. To what in nature does James compare the tongue in 3:7–8? How is this verse convicting? What does it teach about sinful human nature and our ability to control ourselves by our own strength?

10. How does James call out hypocritical uses of the tongue in 3:9–12? According to James, does it seem like any human being is completely free from this kind of doublespeak? Does he offer any hints of hope, with regard to the tongue, for his readers?

11. In what ways does this passage call us to repentance? What truths about God has James already taught, earlier in the letter, that give guidance for how to move forward with this recognition of universal failure in our words and speech?

BIBLE CONNECTIONS

12. While James does not explicitly link the tongue to the heart in this passage, he certainly hints at the tongue's connection to the very essence of who we are. Jesus makes the link more explicitly, with words that are almost certainly in James's mind as he pens his letter. Read Matthew

15:10–20 and note what Jesus says about what comes "out of the mouth." What do Jesus' words add to your understanding of James 3:1–12?

13. Read Proverbs 26:20–22. Where might James have gotten his "fire" imagery for the tongue? How does James expand this image for the tongue and make it even more vivid and powerful?

THEOLOGY CONNECTIONS

14. For Martin Luther, the great Reformer of the sixteenth century, the tongue was certainly a source of great gospel usefulness—but also of great failure! John Piper writes of Luther: "Oh, how many words did Luther regret! This was the downside of a delightfully blunt and open emotional life, filled with humor as well as anger."[1] How does this reality in the life of Luther support James's teaching in 3:1–12? How does it serve as a warning to all of us as Christians?

15. The early church father John Chrysostom once said, "Let us then take this view of the tongue. It is a sword lying in the midst; sharpen it for the

---

1. John Piper, *21 Servants of Sovereign Joy* (Wheaton, IL: Crossway, 2018), 31.

purpose of accusing your own sins. Thrust not the stroke against your brother" (*Instructions to Catechumens*, 1.4). Why is this such important advice? Why might James agree with this proper "sharpening" and use of the tongue, given what you have just studied in James 3:1–12?

APPLYING THE TEXT

16. Consider careless, insensitive, or thoughtless words that you have spoken (perhaps recently), which did damage. What led you to speak those words? How did they reveal something that was in your heart? What is the best way to pray and confront such speech when you stumble in this way?

We Live without Fear, pg. 115

We all stumble and utter words we quickly rue (James 3:1). Yet we strive to please God, whom we love. We do this even if our failures do not jeopardize that love. When we fail, we petition God for grace to renew and purify us, as we appropriate his grace. We live without fear, knowing God will not disown his children for their lapses.

17. In what ways can brothers and sisters in Christ, particularly in the context of the church, hold one another accountable for godly speech and careful use of words? What principles or practices might Christians adopt that could protect them from angry speech, gossip, slander, or careless words?

18. Are there patterns of hypocritical uses of your tongue that you need to confess to God? To others?

PRAYER PROMPT

As we have seen, there is no human being who perfectly reins in and tames the tongue; all of us "stumble in many ways" (3:2). So as you close your study of this passage in James, begin with confession of your sin to God, as you trust the finished and perfect work of Jesus in your place. Our failure should remind us of our need for God's grace; it must lead us to repentance. Then ask God for his strength and Spirit to enable you to bridle your tongue more and more—to use your speech more for his glory and the building up of your brothers and sisters in Christ.

LESSON 9

TWO KINDS OF WISDOM

James 3:13–18

THE BIG PICTURE

As we learned in our study of James 3:1–12 and its focus on the tongue, no one is able to completely control one's speech; we all "stumble" in many ways, as our words so often reflect the sinful nature of our hearts. This reality should drive us in humility to a merciful God, who alone can save us and enable us to live lives of true religion and obedience to him. Now, as we move toward a study of James 3:13–18, we find that James continues to build his case concerning the inherent and natural sinfulness of our hearts and lives. In a way, he is piecing together a kind of indictment of all people, which will lead to a somewhat climactic exhortation in 4:7–10. In the passage for this lesson today, James contrasts two very different kinds of wisdom—the wisdom of God and the wisdom of the world. Following these two different paths brings forth two very different kinds of fruit. Worldly wisdom leads to "bitter jealousy" and "selfish ambition" and is ultimately "demonic" (3:14–15). The wisdom "from above," though, brings forth an entirely different host of fruits, resulting in "a harvest of righteousness" (3:17–18). James calls upon his readers to choose the latter, which can only come to us as a gracious gift from God.

Read James 3:13–18.

GETTING STARTED

1. What are some of the "words of wisdom"—or prevalent mantras—that you hear in the culture around you today? What do they reveal about the most common worldviews of your culture? Consider, for example: "Follow your heart," "You do you," and "Believe in yourself."

2. What immediately comes to mind when you hear the word *wisdom*? How would you go about judging whether or not a person—or a piece of advice—is truly wise?

OBSERVING THE TEXT

3. What repeated words or phrases does James use in this passage? What does this suggest is the main point of this part of his letter?

God's Wisdom Comes Down, pg. 119

God does not leave us to ourselves. Before he develops his indictment of human sin in full, he presents two ways of life. We *should* choose the way of wisdom, yet we do not have the power in ourselves to do so. So, by grace, God's wisdom comes down to us.

4. As you probably noticed in your initial reading, this passage consists mainly of an extended contrast between two different systems of wisdom. How does James label and categorize these two different kinds of wisdom?

5. What are the contrasting results, or fruits, that come from these two competing systems of wisdom, according to James? What do you notice about the specific fruits that he chooses to mention for each kind of wisdom?

UNDERSTANDING THE TEXT

6. How does the passage you are studying today follow logically from the passage you studied in the past lesson (James 3:1–12)? What case does James seem to be building in chapter 3?

7. What do you notice about the shape of this passage? (Hint: consider how 3:13 and 3:17–18 are similar, in contrast to 3:14–16.) What does James seem to be emphasizing, given the structure of these verses?

8. According to 3:13, what kind of a life results from a commitment to wisdom? How does "meekness" contrast with the descriptions, actions, and attitudes that follow in 3:14–16?

9. What are the fruits, or results, of wisdom that is *not* from above, according to James 3:14–16? Why might this be? Why do you think he chooses to mention these specific sins and vices in these verses?

10. Why might James still refer to earthly wisdom as a kind of "wisdom" (3:15)? How might worldly approaches to wisdom have a kind of order and logic to them? What might this look like?

The Excellent Life, pg. 121
What James calls "the wisdom that comes from heaven" drives the excellent life. The wise demonstrate God's wisdom daily. They inspire others by giving them a living model of righteousness that incarnates the will of God. Their lives become models of righteousness.

11. In 3:18, James's concluding comments about God's wisdom have to do with its final benefits and results; this peace-loving wisdom of God produces "a harvest of righteousness." How might living according to God's wisdom have disproportionate effects beyond one's own individual life? What other Scriptures might James have in mind as he writes these words?

BIBLE CONNECTIONS

12. As we have mentioned before, James's letter often draws from the Wisdom Literature of the Scriptures, calling our minds back to books like Proverbs. Take a moment to glance over Proverbs 1:20–33, noting what is said about the call of wisdom, which is personified in that passage. How might this picture have informed James as he contrasted earthly wisdom with wisdom from above?

13. James's picture of wisdom that is "sown" and produces "a harvest" is connected to many other agricultural metaphors used in Scripture to describe the beautiful and blessed growth that results from a faithful and godly life. Consider Mark 4:1–9, Jesus' parable of the sower. According to Jesus, what is the result of rightly hearing and receiving the Word of God?

THEOLOGY CONNECTIONS

14. John Calvin famously begins his *Institutes of the Christian Religion* by stressing the starting point for true wisdom: "Our wisdom, in so far as it ought to be deemed true and solid Wisdom, consists almost entirely of two parts: the knowledge of God and of ourselves." How does this assertion from Calvin agree with what James writes about wisdom? In what ways do various forms of earthly wisdom fail in these two basic foundations of true knowledge that Calvin identifies?

15. While the Westminster Confession of Faith asserts the perspicuity (clarity) of Scripture, it also affirms that accepting and believing God's Word comes as a gift from him: "We acknowledge the inward illumination of the Spirit of God to be necessary for the saving understanding of such things as are revealed in the Word" (1.6). What has James already insisted about the right attitude toward God's Word? What must God do for us, according to James (and according to the Westminster Confession of Faith), in order to grant us access to knowledge and life according to his wisdom from above?

APPLYING THE TEXT

16. In what ways might you detect how significantly you are affected and guided by earthly wisdom, rather than wisdom from heaven? How

might certain fruits in your life (such as jealousy, bitterness, and selfish ambition) alert you to this dynamic?

17. How might you seek to cultivate peace and meekness in your heart and life? What practices, disciplines, or patterns of prayer might enable you to grow in those fruits of heavenly wisdom?

18. What was convicting about this passage, as you considered the two competing systems of wisdom that James puts forward? How might you invite God to impart his wisdom to you with more power in the coming days?

The Fruits of Godly Wisdom, pg. 126
The effect of these traits of wisdom is peace and righteousness for the family of God (3:18). If earthly wisdom brings strife, the wise man brings unity and peace. . . . Indeed, God fashioned us to flourish in an atmosphere of peace.

PRAYER PROMPT

As you saw in James's conclusion to this passage (3:18), a life permeated with God's wisdom is not for our benefit only; it produces "a harvest of righteousness" that should bless and encourage people around us. Pray today that as you submit in faith and repentance to God, his wisdom would shape your life and allow you to bless, serve, and encourage others. Ask him to use your life to produce a "harvest" of his righteousness in the lives of people in your family, church, and community.

LESSON 10

THE GOSPEL
ACCORDING TO JAMES

James 4:1–6

THE BIG PICTURE

James has just presented a very stark contrast between the wisdom of the world and the wisdom "from above" (3:13–18). Now, as chapter 4 begins, James will expand his warnings against an unhealthy and unholy relationship with the sinful world and its wisdom. While worldly wisdom leads to many unhealthy dynamics in our relationships (4:1–2), it is ultimately rooted in a self-obsessed spirit of pride. The sinful world, in contrast to God, urges its servants to put themselves first; their lives become bent on self-fulfillment, self-gratification, and the indulgence of all of their pleasures and desires (4:2–3). What results is an ugly, covetous, contentious, and ultimately unfulfilling journey that leads to nothing but death—not to mention enmity with God (4:4). According to James, there is only one way out of such worldly striving and sin: finding grace with God through humility and submission to him (4:6–7). Indeed, humility will mark the lives of those who love God, for he grants grace to such as these.

Read James 4:1–6.

GETTING STARTED

1. If you have had the opportunity to observe people who pursue pleasure and self-gratification rather than God, what have you noticed about the impact of these pursuits on their human relationships? Why is there so often relational "collateral damage" when people turn from God to an obsession with self?

2. What kind of "internal battles" have you fought with yourself in recent years? What kind of competing desires tend to "wage war" within you? Describe these battles, which could have to do with spiritual problems, or with issues of time management, exercise, or diet, or with relationships, or even with patterns of thought.

The Fruits of Earthly Wisdom, pg. 131

James 4:1 says worldly wisdom leads to fights and struggles. James says there are fights "*among* you" because of passions "that are at war *within* you." . . . Selfish passions make believers wage war within themselves, as their desire to serve Christ and neighbor conflicts with the desire to serve self.

OBSERVING THE TEXT

3. At first glance, James's questions in 3:13 and 4:1 do not seem to be related. But, given James's contrast between worldly wisdom and God's wisdom in 3:13–18, how might they be connected? What does James mention in 4:1 that is similar to what he has mentioned before (in 3:14–16)?

4. James makes some strong assertions about the internal struggles that go on inside of each of us. What are some of the claims he makes regarding our desires, passions, and internal battles?

5. How does James continue his contrast between the world and God in this passage? What seem to be the main differences in behavior between those who are friends of the world and those who are friends of God (4:4–6)?

UNDERSTANDING THE TEXT

6. How do we often use the word *passion* in a positive sense in our culture today? How does James seem to be using this word in 4:1? What are

the results of the kinds of "passions" that are at war within each one of us? What does this teach us about our sinful nature?

7. In 4:2, what does James suggest that we ought to do about our desires and wants? Why is this such a better alternative than fighting and quarreling? What might James be suggesting that we often forget about God?

8. According to James 4:3, there is a wrong way to ask God about our desires. What wrong motivations do we sometimes bring to our prayers, according to James?

9. What does the phrase "adulterous people" imply about James's understanding of his readers' relationship with God (4:4)? In what ways might "friendship with the world" be likened to spiritual "adultery," in the way James is describing it?

Spiritual Adultery, pg. 134

When James says, "You adulterous people," he makes a specific accusation. The charge is spiritual adultery, not spiritual fornication, because the people are joined to Christ. They are married to Jesus, but they run after other gods.

10. The quotation in James 4:5 (which is not a direct quotation of any Old Testament passage) is notoriously difficult to translate. It is probably best to understand the "spirit" as the human spirit, which is also the main subject of the sentence. If this is the case, James would be summarizing the human condition, explaining how our spirits are constantly prone to envy, jealousy, and an undying yearning to please ourselves. How is this a good summary of the human condition? How could this explain much of human history, including the rise and fall of leaders and nations?

11. How might James 4:6 offer the solution to the sinful battle within every human soul? How does this verse direct us to respond? What does it tell us about God, and how is it a hopeful verse to conclude this passage?

BIBLE CONNECTIONS

12. As we saw, James 4:5 can be taken a few different ways. Some scholars interpret it as describing God's jealous yearning to have people love and serve him; others see it better understood as a description of the sinfully envious yearning of the human spirit, which pursues sin and selfish gratification. Take a moment and read 2 Timothy 3:1–5, and consider Paul's description of those who love themselves and pursue

pleasure at all costs. How might one see 2 Timothy 3:1–5 as a fuller picture of the envious yearning of the human spirit apart from Christ?

13. When James calls out his audience as "adulterous," he is using well-worn language from the Old Testament prophets. Look at Isaiah 57:2–3, 8, and note the prophet's vivid description of the faithlessness of God's people. Why is Isaiah's language particularly poignant? How does it expand our understanding of the sin of God's people?

THEOLOGY CONNECTIONS

14. The Westminster Confession of Faith explains that growth in sanctification will occur in every believer, but it will be "imperfect in this life, there abiding still some remnants of corruption in every part; whence ariseth a continual and irreconcilable war, the flesh lusting against the Spirit, and the Spirit against the flesh" (13.2). How does this "war" language connect with the passage in James that you have just studied?

15. Given what you know about the doctrine of salvation, why might James point to humility as the main characteristic of those who obtain grace from God? How is humility inextricably linked to repentance? How

ought a right understanding of justification cause humility? Why is faith in the substitutionary death of Jesus impossible without humility?

APPLYING THE TEXT

16. Given what James says about "quarrels" and "fights" among Christians (4:1), how might you examine your own heart the next time you are in conflict with another Christian? How might this passage help you with humility in the midst of an argument or disagreement?

17. What internal battles or struggles has this text helped you to identify in your own heart? What areas of your life—or desires and pursuits—could perhaps be described as involving "friendship with the world" (4:4)?

God Will Give Grace, pg. 139

If we do find such sins, we should take them to God and confess them to him. Then, James promises, God will give grace to the humble. James does not here specify what that means, but the rest of the Scripture tells us.

18. In what ways do you need to be reminded of the prerequisite of humility in your relationship with God? How can you pursue the kind of humility to which God responds with grace?

PRAYER PROMPT

Like many of the passages we have studied in the book of James, this one ought to highlight specific sins that plague our lives—or at least cause internal battles in our hearts. Take a moment to confess these sins to God. Where might there be relational conflict in your life right now, and what sinful desires in your heart might have had a role in creating that conflict? How might you be enjoying friendship with the world in a way that is adulterous, given your covenant relationship with God? As you confess these sins, ask humbly for God's forgiveness, knowing that he is the God who gives grace, through his Son, to the humble.

Skims over the section 13-17.
Misses the point.
We all do this. ∧ (A lot.) Most procrastination
is an arrogant presumption that,
"Oh, I can do
that later." Then time runs out & we

LESSON 11

HUMILITY AND PRIDE

fail in
our duty
to those
who are
depending
on us.

James 4:5–17

THE BIG PICTURE

The passage that you studied in your last lesson—James 4:1–6—concluded with a kind of summary of the story of sinful humanity, whose spirits constantly envy others and pursue pleasure and self-gratification apart from Christ. There was also a point of hope in 4:6—that God "gives grace to the humble." Now, as James continues, he will explain more about the beauty of a life that is characterized by humility, repentance, and submission to God. While God opposes those who are proud, he does indeed offer grace to the humble sinners who submit themselves to him (4:6–7). When we weep over our sins with repentance, we can trust in being ultimately exalted by God (4:10). God's people begin not only to repent with humility, but also to treat one another with humility; they reject judgmental attitudes and trust God to act as the final judge of others (4:11–12). These attitudes and actions stand in stark contrast to the pride, arrogance, and boasting of those who reject God and claim to control their own destiny (4:13). The humble follower who knows God's grace entrusts himself or herself to the will of God, knowing the brevity of life and the eternal importance of submission to him.

Read James 4:5–17.

GETTING STARTED

1. What are some examples that you've seen of people apologizing for something only after they have been caught? Why does that make you question the sincerity of their apology and confession? What are some ways in which you can tell if someone is truly sorry for a wrong that he or she has committed?

2. Give some examples of bold plans that people make for their lives, businesses, futures, or family goals. In what ways are you tempted to think that you control your own future and destiny, rather than God? What is the danger of such thinking?

The Gift of Humility, pg. 144

In one sense, even humility is God's gift. No one rejects his pride unless the Lord enables him. The Lord opens eyes so men and women can see the futility of living for themselves. Grace teaches us to trust in God, to rest in Christ, rather than the self. So James commands us to humble ourselves before God.

OBSERVING THE TEXT

3. Given some of the actions and attitudes that James confronts in this passage, what can you learn—or assume—about his audience? What tendencies do they have, and to what sinful ways of thinking and acting are they prone?

4. What are the contrasting actions and attitudes that James highlights in 4:5–17? What does the arrogant person tend to do and say? How do humble people tend to act? How do both types of people approach or act toward God?

5. Note the many straightforward commands (imperatives) that James gives in this passage. What are some of these commands? What do they tell you about what is most important to James?

UNDERSTANDING THE TEXT

6. What are some of the characteristics and actions associated with true humility, according to James 4:7–10? What does James seem to be

teaching in these verses about the proper response to God? Why does he call his audience to "be wretched" and to "weep" (4:9), and what does he mean by those instructions?

7. What does it mean to "submit yourself" to God (4:7)? How does that word carry a negative connotation in our culture today, but why is it such a positive word for James with regard to our relationship with God? How is resisting the devil related to submission to God (4:7)?

8. What do verses 8–10 of this passage teach us about the way we approach God? What do we learn about the reality of human sinfulness? What hopeful and encouraging truths for repentant sinners does James mention regarding the character and nature of God?

Good News for the Humble, pg. 152
If we humble ourselves, if we admit that we sin, and that we are sinful, and that we cannot reform ourselves, then, James promises, the Lord will lift us up. This is the gospel according to James.

9. How do verses 11–12 fit into the broader context of James's teaching about humility and pride? In what ways might humility and submission to God cut into our tendencies to be judgmental? How might genuine repentance and sorrow for our sin lead us to be merciful, patient, and gracious toward our neighbor?

10. What is the attitude that James seems to be confronting in 4:13? Is he teaching that planning for the future is evil? If not, what exactly is boastful and arrogant about the plans of the people he confronts (4:16)?

See note at opening of chapter.

11. How does James seek to remind his readers of the brevity and fragility of human life (4:14)? Why is this a helpful reminder, and how ought this realization to affect our attitudes and prayers? How is this related to the humility and submission that James has just discussed (4:7–10)?

BIBLE CONNECTIONS

12. There is perhaps no better or richer model of wretched, mournful, and humble repentance than David's confession in Psalm 51. Take a minute

and read that psalm. How do you see James's instructions in 4:7–10 followed and practiced perfectly by King David? What else do you notice about David's heartfelt declaration of repentance before God?

13. The one psalm written by Moses, Psalm 90, seems to echo many of James's themes in 4:13–16. Read Psalm 90:1–6, 12–17, noting Moses' realistic description of the brevity of human life. How does Moses conclude? How is his conclusion to Psalm 90 similar to James's exhortation in 4:15?

THEOLOGY CONNECTIONS

14. The Heidelberg Catechism describes repentance and the "dying of the old nature" with these words: "It is to grieve with heartfelt sorrow that we have offended God by our sin, and more and more to hate it and flee from it" (Q&A 89). How does this description of true repentance echo the words of James (particularly in 4:8–10)?

15. The Scots Confession, written mainly by the great Reformer John Knox, opens with an unashamed acclamation of God's sovereignty, omnipotence, and providence over everything that happens. We serve

a God, Knox writes, who rules the world and our lives according to his "inscrutable providence" (art. 1). If this is indeed true, why must James's instructions in 4:16 be so carefully and humbly heeded?

APPLYING THE TEXT

16. In what ways should humility and submission characterize your relationship with God more than is currently the case? How can you seek to identify patterns of pride that may get in the way of your humble confession of sin and mournful repentance before him?

17. How do you tend to use your words to judge or slander others (4:11–12)? If you detect judgmental and slanderous tendencies within your heart (and coming from your mouth), how can you work to change them? What hidden attitudes and dispositions might lead to judgmental thoughts or words, and why are these problematic (see John 7:24)?

18. Obviously, planning for the future is not sinful; it is prudent! But how can our thinking about our future sometimes be done without any consideration of God? What might this look like in your life right now, and how might this tendency betray hidden pride or arrogance?

PRAYER PROMPT

Perhaps the best way to pray, coming out of your study of this passage in James, is to ask God for deeper humility and submission to him. Ask him to help you "mourn" over your sins and failure. Pray that he would strengthen you to trust his will—and protect you from sinful ambition and boastful arrogance about your future plans. Most of all, humble yourself before him, knowing that in Christ he will forgive your sins and lift you up.

Responding to God's Good Guidance, pg. 155
The achiever may think, "But I have worked hard to hone my skills." Perhaps so. But even then, we can ask if God did not guide our desires and nudge us toward godly aspirations. So let us ever be humble, rejoice in God's goodness, and use our gifts for him.

LESSON 12

WOE TO THE RICH

James 5:1–6

THE BIG PICTURE

While chapter 5 of the book of James introduces a new subject—riches and wealth—it is a subject that is next in James's natural progression of thought, as he confronts the effects of worldly wisdom on our lives. As we have already seen, many sinful attitudes and actions can be traced back to pride and envy: quarrels, anger, misuse of speech, judgmentalism, arrogance, and a general lack of humility and repentance. Now, in the first six verses of chapter 5, we find that worldly wisdom also leads to gross misuse of wealth—and even to the oppression of others in order to gain more wealth. James rails against those who have heaped up treasures for themselves in this life, and particularly those who have done so through deception, unfair business practices, and the oppression of others (5:4). Such people have lived lives of complete self-indulgence and the pursuit of pleasure; many have even been guilty of the murder of righteous people—either directly or indirectly (5:5–6). Ultimately, for James, such abuse of wealth reveals a lack of humility. The rich who hoard and oppress have failed to submit themselves to God; their god is their money, and they will squash anyone who gets in the way of their accumulation.

Read James 5:1–6.

GETTING STARTED

1. What approaches to riches, wealth, and possessions have you observed in the Christian community and church? How have you observed different people use the Bible to back up very different perspectives on how much we should own, how much we should make, or how much we ought to give away?

2. How have sinful attitudes about money, or the accumulation of possessions, crept into your circles of friends or acquaintances? In what ways can our commercial culture, with its view of accumulation, comfort, wealth, and materialism, infect even the church?

OBSERVING THE TEXT

3. What are the initial surprises in this passage, which may have struck you as you read it through?

The Final Mark of a Worldly Wise Life, pg. 164

When James denounces hoarding, oppression, indulgence, and financial violence, he is not simply denouncing several random acts of wickedness. Abuse of wealth is the final mark of a life of worldly "wisdom" James describes in 3:13–4:3. Abuse of wealth is another form of envy, coveting, strife, and grasping.

4. How does James's tone, and the general manner with which he addresses his audience, change in these verses? How would you contrast his tone with the way he addressed his readers earlier in the letter (see, for example, James's addressing of "brothers" throughout chapter 2)?

5. What are some of the characteristics and actions of the rich people whom James addresses in these verses? What is it about their behavior that seems to make James most incensed? Does he seem to think these rich people are Christians and part of the church? Why or why not?

UNDERSTANDING THE TEXT

6. Based on the opening verses of this passage (5:1–3), why might you argue that James is speaking mainly to wealthy people who are *not* genuine Christians? How does he address them (5:1), and how is this different from titles he has used before in the letter? What does James seem to anticipate about their future judgment?

7. What has happened to the riches and possessions of those who have hoarded them, according to what James says in 5:2–3? What warnings are implicit in the descriptions in these verses? How might James be subtly teaching about right investments and an eternal perspective on our possessions?

8. According to 5:4, what kind of treatment of people has played a major part in the growing wealth of the rich people James denounces? How does James introduce the presence of God into this verse?

9. While James 5:5 does not condemn wealth and possessions per se, what kind of attitudes and motivations does he denounce in the lives and hearts of wealthy people? What seems to be driving the men and women whom James confronts?

Dangerous Undertow, pg. 169
James's warning to the rich is, properly speaking, irrelevant for believers. We live for God, not wealth. Yet we need these warnings. Whenever we forget the gospel of God's love and grace, the undertow of the world's values threatens to sweep us away.

10. For at least some of the wealthy people that James has in view, their sinful behavior has not stopped at self-indulgence, or even at the oppression of the poor. What additional sins does James decry in 5:6? How does he characterize the "righteous" person who falls prey to the violence of the sinful rich person?

BIBLE CONNECTIONS

11. In James 5:1–6, you have studied verses that one could almost mistake for a passage from the Old Testament prophets. Many prophets of God railed against the rich oppressors of his people, promising God's eventual relief for the poor and judgment on the cruel and wealthy rulers. Read Micah 2:1–3, for example, and note tones and themes similar to those in James 5:1–6. What do you notice? What does Micah identify as sin, and what does he promise regarding God's judgment?

12. Read Revelation 18:9–13. From these verses, what seems to be the appeal of "Babylon" for many of the world's leaders and merchants? What warnings about the sinful pursuit of wealth and possessions are implicit in that passage in Revelation? How might they reinforce James's confrontation in 5:1–6?

THEOLOGY CONNECTIONS

13. Martin Luther once remarked, "Wealth is the smallest thing on earth, the least gift that God has bestowed on mankind" (*Table Talk*, trans. Hazlitt, 67). What might Luther be suggesting about the value of riches in God's economy? Why might there be far greater gifts—spiritually speaking—that God might see fit to bestow on his children? How has James pointed to this reality earlier in his letter?

14. The Puritan preacher Jonathan Edwards once vigorously confronted the way that material wealth was overvalued in the church: "Some have more stately houses than others, and some are in higher office than others, and some are richer than others and have higher seats in the meeting house than others; but all graves are upon a level. One rotting, putrefying corpse is as ignoble as another; the worms are as bold with one carcass as another" ("Many Mansions," 1737). What connections do you see between Edwards's words and James 5:1–3?

? But they are in the church too. Some wheat that need to repent. Some tares — not true believers.

APPLYING THE TEXT

15. While we have seen that James is most likely directing his words in this passage primarily to the unbelieving wealthy oppressors of our world, there are certainly implicit warnings for Christians about our tendency to love wealth, money, possessions, and material things more

than God. What warnings did you personally take from James 5:1–6 regarding wealth? How might you need to adjust your attitude toward your material possessions?

16. In what practical ways might you seek to loosen your grip on money, wealth, and possessions, and pursue even more humble reliance upon God? How can you encourage the Christians around you to do the same?

17. How does the gospel of God's grace through Jesus Christ free us from reliance on power, money, and "success" in the eyes of the world? In what ways *must* our submission to God and faith in him change our priorities and our greatest treasure?

Longing for Life with God, pg. 173

By faith, believers are prepared and remain prepared for that day [of God's judgment]. When our hearts are right, we long for it. So then, let us not live like the godless rich, who grasp, hoard, and indulge themselves. Let us live out the conviction that the riches of this age are fleeting, and that our life with God is forever rewarding.

PRAYER PROMPT

It is impossible for people who are gripped by a love of money to change their hearts—unless the Holy Spirit enables repentance, humility, and the experience of a far greater joy and treasure in God himself. Today, as you conclude your study of James 5:1–6, ask God to free you from the love of money. Pray that he would grant you humility, repentance, and eternal joy and pleasure in him, as you follow Jesus Christ your Savior.

LESSON 13

ENDURANCE AND HEALING

James 5:7–20

THE BIG PICTURE

As we end our time of study in the book of James with a rather large passage (5:7–20), which includes several different themes and commands, it is good to remember the structure of the final two chapters. The passage today concludes a section of the letter that began in 4:11–12 with a warning from James to refrain from using our *words* in judgmental ways toward a brother or sister. The section concludes at 5:19–20 with an exhortation to use *words* in a wholesome way—to lovingly call back a brother or sister from sin. In between those two bookends, James calls his readers to prayer and trust (5:13–18), rather than arrogant planning (4:13–16), while warning rich oppressors (5:1–6) and comforting those who patiently wait for God's judgment (5:7–11). In other words, there is a shape to these final chapters of James, even though they can appear to be unrelated commands fired off in quick succession. In this passage, James calls Christians to humble patience as they wait for the coming of the Lord, as well as earnest and faith-filled prayer in the midst of suffering while they wait.

Read James 5:7–20.

GETTING STARTED

1. Give some examples of times when you have had to be reminded to be patient. What tends to make you impatient? What are the negative effects of impatience on your own heart—and also on relationships with those around you?

2. In what ways do Christians tend to struggle in the midst of sickness and physical suffering—either in their own lives or in the lives of those close to them? What questions do they ask about the right way to pray? What mistakes do we tend to make in the midst of sickness and suffering?

OBSERVING THE TEXT

3. How might a concern for patience flow logically out of what James has just written in 5:1–6? How might a patient person approach life differently than the rich people James has just addressed? Why might those who have been victims of rich oppressors need to be reminded to embrace patience?

4. What are your initial observations about the final fourteen verses of the book of James? What themes emerge that James has mentioned before? What new ideas are introduced?

5. What strikes you about James's teaching on suffering, prayer, and healing (5:13–20)? How have you seen these verses used and/or followed in your church context or tradition?

UNDERSTANDING THE TEXT

6. James uses several different, yet related, words as he calls upon his Christian audience to patiently wait for the coming judgment of God. He tells them to be "patient" (5:7–8), to "establish" their hearts, or stand firm (5:8), and to remain "steadfast," or persevere (5:11). How are these words helpful, when used together, in forming a picture of the kind of Christians that James wants us to be? What subtly different meanings might these words carry?

When We Face Oppression, pg. 178
After James describes the arrogance of the rich and self-indulgent oppressors, he names their fate at the hands of the Judge. When the family of God faces oppression, we must neither grumble nor seek vengeance. We must remain patient until the Lord comes. We will remember the lessons that the proud forget.

7. What does James suggest about the coming of the Lord (5:8–9)? How are we to interpret his statements about the Lord's coming, and how is James speaking in similar ways as other parts of the New Testament? What commands does James give (and what examples does he use) to guide our behavior in light of the imminence of the Lord's return?

8. How might 5:12—James's command about oaths—be linked to his instructions about patience in the midst of trials and waiting for the Lord's return? How might this command connect to James's call to humility? What wrong attitudes or practices with regard to oath-taking might James be confronting?

9. What does James seem to be suggesting, in 5:13, about the proper times and occasions for prayer in the Christian life? How do prayers—in every season—demonstrate our humility and submission to God?

The Prayers of the Righteous, pg. 200

James expects those prayers to be effective, for "the prayer of a righteous man is powerful and effective" (5:16). Elders are responsible to set an example of personal righteousness, yet James 5:16 expects the whole church to pray. Every saint—everyone who is righteous by faith—prays.

10. What kind of situation seems to be in James's mind as he gives his instructions about special, elder-led prayer and anointing (5:14–15)? What is the context for this kind of prayer, and what are James's specific instructions? What does 5:16 seem to suggest about the potential role of sin in issues of physical suffering that require prayer?

11. How does James demonstrate the power of effective prayer in 5:17–18? What point is he making to his readers? How do the final verses of James—5:19–20—connect to the previous discussion of effective prayer in the context of believers? In what way do those verses call the church to pray—and act—for the good of healthy hearts, lives, and souls?

BIBLE CONNECTIONS

12. Like Paul, Peter, and even Jesus himself, James urges his audience to treat the coming of the Lord as *imminent*—that is, we are to live and think as if Jesus could return at any hour. Read James 5:8–9 again, and then compare these verses with the teaching of Jesus in Mark 13:32–37. How is James's teaching similar to that of Jesus about his return?

13. In James 5:16, as you saw, James seems to suggest that, at least some-times, different kinds of suffering can be linked to unconfessed sin. Read Psalm 32:1–5. What are the distinctly physical effects of unconfessed sin that David mentions in these verses? How does he describe relief and healing finally coming to him?

THEOLOGY CONNECTIONS

14. The Westminster Confession of Faith affirms that Jesus Christ intends to "have that day unknown to men, that they may shake off all carnal security, and be always watchful, because they know not at what hour the Lord will come; and may be ever prepared to say, Come Lord Jesus, come quickly" (33.3). How do James's words about the coming of the Lord agree with the WCF on this point? How is it possible to be both patient and watchful with regard to Christ's return?

15. While James certainly lifts up faithful prayer as effective (and required!), it would not be a faithful interpretation of James 5:16–20 to suggest that *every* prayer in the midst of sickness will result in physical healing. R. C. Sproul suggests that such an expectation actually places ourselves above God: "Prayer is not magic. God is not a celestial bellhop ready at our beck and call to satisfy our every whim. In some cases our prayers must involve travail of the soul and agony of heart such as Jesus himself

experienced in the Garden."[1] When we pray with faith, how must we also submit ourselves to the will of a sovereign God?

APPLYING THE TEXT

16. Do you struggle with impatience when you see injustice, oppression, and abuse? If so, why? Why is it good to long for God's justice? Why must we embrace an attitude of patience and endurance as we wait for Christ's return?

17. What prevents you from praying when you are cheerful? What prevents you from praying when you are sick or suffering? How and when might you counsel a sick or suffering brother or sister to seek special prayer from the elders of your church?

1. R. C. Sproul, *Does Prayer Change Things?* (North Mankato, MN: Reformation Trust, 2009), part 14 (ePub).

18. How might you prepare to use your words to bring back a "wandering" sinner who is close to you (5:19–20)? What needs to be your motivation in pursuing a person who is wandering from the Lord? Does this need to happen in any relationship in your life currently?

PRAYER PROMPT

As James nears the end of his letter, he uses some of his final words to call his audience to pray—in every situation of life! Today, as you look back on your study of James 5:7–20, first pray for patience, endurance, and resilience as you live faithfully for Jesus Christ and await his return. Pray that you would not hold tightly to unconfessed sin, but humbly bring it before the merciful and compassionate Savior. Finally, ask God for greater faith to approach him with confidence—in every situation of life.

Concluding the Epistle, pg. 204

These final thoughts of James unite several themes of his epistle. To pursue a sinner in order to win him to Christ is a proper response to a trial (James 1:2–12). It is a form of kindness to a brother (2:14–26), a proper use of speech (3:1–12), and it leads people to humble themselves before the Lord (4:6–10).

Jon Nielson is senior pastor of Spring Valley Presbyterian Church in Roselle, Illinois, and the author of *Bible Study: A Student's Guide*, among other books. He has served in pastoral positions at Holy Trinity Church, Chicago, and College Church, Wheaton, Illinois, and as director of training for the Charles Simeon Trust.

Daniel M. Doriani (PhD, Westminster Theological Seminary; STM, Yale Divinity School) is vice president of strategic academic projects and professor of theology at Covenant Theological Seminary. Previously he was senior pastor of Central Presbyterian Church in Clayton, Missouri.

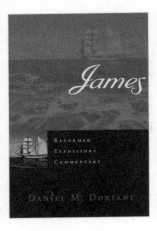

Although James may not articulate the doctrine of atonement through the death and resurrection of Jesus, he does present Christ in his own way, and his wisdom is rooted in grace. Daniel Doriani, a pastor and scholar recognized for his works on biblical interpretation and application, show us how.

Praise for the Reformed Expository Commentary Series

"Well-researched and well-reasoned, practical and pastoral, shrewd, solid, and searching." —**J. I. Packer**

"A rare combination of biblical insight, theological substance, and pastoral application." —**Al Mohler**

"Here, rigorous expository methodology, nuanced biblical theology, and pastoral passion combine." —**R. Kent Hughes**